About This Resource

Why is this topic important?

When people have competing claims, it is very difficult for them to be open to each other's needs and concerns. Often people try to circumvent the discomfort of addressing conflict in an open way, attempting instead to force their solutions on others or avoid the conflict entirely. This program helps participants to use a more effective approach.

What can you achieve with this resource?

This is a guide for the person who wishes to facilitate a training program that teaches individuals to resolve conflict effectively. It is based on the premise that reaching, or even attempting to reach, a win/win solution requires a willing and active attempt to understand the other person's stated—and unstated—needs. This program is intended for any participants who experience work-related conflict with virtually anyone, from colleague to customer, from direct report to one's own boss.

Although brief, the program is not a leader-centered presentation or merely an hour of group discussion. Instead, participants are engaged in short activities that heighten their awareness of their current attitudes and behaviors, inspire them to adopt new ones, and provide them with concrete suggestions that can be used immediately back on the job.

How is this resource organized?

The training program can be conducted in one hour (the length can be extended with a more leisurely pace) without making concessions to the extra time that participatory training sessions usually require. It features "active training" techniques in which lecturing is minimized and learning activity is maximized. The 60-minute format allows the facilitator to provide effective training in a brief time period. As a result, busy employees can attend a training session without disrupting their work day. The active training techniques used in this program are designed to increase participation, enliven learning, deepen retention, and encourage application.

The program can be conducted with as few as four participants and yet also functions well for a larger group. Participants can be drawn from different parts of an organization or be members of an intact team.

About Pfeiffer

Pfeiffer serves the professional development and hands-on resource needs of training and human resource practitioners and gives them products to do their jobs better. We deliver proven ideas and solutions from experts in HR development and HR management, and we offer effective and customizable tools to improve workplace performance. From novice to seasoned professional, Pfeiffer is the source you can trust to make yourself and your organization more successful.

Essential Knowledge Pfeiffer produces insightful, practical, and comprehensive materials on topics that matter the most to training and HR professionals. Our Essential Knowledge resources translate the expertise of seasoned professionals into practical, how-to guidance on critical workplace issues and problems. These resources are supported by case studies, worksheets, and job aids and are frequently supplemented with CD-ROMs, websites, and other means of making the content easier to read, understand, and use.

Essential Tools Pfeiffer's Essential Tools resources save time and expense by offering proven, ready-to-use materials—including exercises, activities, games, instruments, and assessments—for use during a training or team-learning event. These resources are frequently offered in looseleaf or CD-ROM format to facilitate copying and customization of the material.

Pfeiffer also recognizes the remarkable power of new technologies in expanding the reach and effectiveness of training. While e-hype has often created whizbang solutions in search of a problem, we are dedicated to bringing convenience and enhancements to proven training solutions. All our e-tools comply with rigorous functionality standards. The most appropriate technology wrapped around essential content yields the perfect solution for today's on-the-go trainers and human resource professionals.

Pfeiffer
www.pfeiffer.com

Essential resources for training and HR professionals

Other 60-Minute Active Training Series Titles

The 60-Minute Active Training Series

HOW TO RESOLVE CONFLICT EFFECTIVELY

LEADER'S
GUIDE

Mel Silberman and Freda Hansburg

For additional copies/bulk purchases of this book in the U.S. please contact 800-274-4434.

Pfeiffer books and products are available through most bookstores. To contact Pfeiffer directly call our Customer Care Department within the U.S. at 800-274-4434, outside the U.S. at 317-572-3985 or fax 317-572-4002 or www.pfeiffer.com.

Pfeiffer also publishes its books in a variety of electronic formats. Some content that appears in print may not be available in electronic books.

ISBN: 0-7879-7351-3

Acquiring Editor: Martin Delahoussaye   Senior Production Editor: Dawn Kilgore

Director of Development: Kathleen Dolan Davies   Manufacturing Supervisor: Becky Carreno

Developmental Editor: Susan Rachmeler   Interior Design: Erin Zeltner

Editor: Rebecca Taff

Printed in the United States of America

Printing 10   9   8   7   6   5   4   3   2   1

CONTENTS

Getting the Most from This Resource

In today's organizations, more work is done by fewer people, the pace is fast, and immediate results are expected. As a result, a classroom-delivered training program lasting several hours, if not days, is a luxury not always affordable.

One solution is to replace classroom instruction with self-directed e-learning. While this approach is very helpful, it is not the only option. Briefer classroom training also makes sense . . . if the session is highly focused and the pace is accelerated.

You can introduce "60-minute" training by finding a convenient time for a group to assemble. It may be during lunch (as in a "lunch and learn" format), at the beginning or end of the work day, or at any time when a break from "business as usual" may be welcomed. Moreover, the training can be worthwhile with a group as small as four participants. The program can be delivered to much larger groups, as well.

This 60-minute program utilizes a training approach described in the book *Active Training* (Silberman, 1998). The goals of active training are

- To Increase Participation

- To Enliven Learning

- To Deepen Retention

- To Encourage Application

An active approach to training is based on the idea that it's not what *we tell* participants that counts; it's what *they take away*. Learning is not an automatic consequence of pouring information into another person's head. It requires the learner's own mental involvement and doing. Therefore, lecturing should be minimized and learning activity should be maximized.

To increase the chances that participants *take away* a lot, even in a short period of time, this 60-minute active training program has been designed with five key ingredients in mind.

1. Moderate Level of Content

This training session concentrates on critical learning areas—those elements of the subject that provide the essential basis on which to build later. In designing training sessions, the tendency too often is to cover the waterfront by throwing in everything possible about a given subject. After all, you only get one shot at these participants, so you'd better make sure you have covered it all. You may fail to realize, however, that participants will forget far more than they will ever learn. The best approach is to be selective, choosing the "need to know" before the "nice to know." Training sessions that promote active learning have a lean curriculum.

2. Variety of Learning Methods

This training series employs an assortment of learning methods from *101 Ways to Make Training Active*, 2nd ed. (Silberman, 2005). They include self-assessment scales, experiential exercises, small group discussion, role play, and lecturettes. A variety of training approaches keeps interest alive and can help minimize the downtimes when energy levels are low. Another and even more important argument for variety is that adults learn in different ways. Using different learning approaches is likely to be more effective than a single approach that may work for some but not for others.

3. Opportunities for Group Participation

This training session promotes active involvement of participants by utilizing interactive whole group formats, pair discussion/activity, and small group activities. Group participation has advantages in any training session. Involving the group moves training from the passive to the active. Group activity engages participants in the learning process and makes them working partners with the trainer.

4. Utilization of Participants' Experience

Each participant in a training program brings relevant experiences to the session. Some of these experiences will be directly applicable; others may involve analogies from previous jobs or situations. In either case, much of the learning in this training session comes from one's peers.

5. Encouragement of "Back on the Job" Application

At the conclusion of any training session, participants will naturally ask "Now what?" The success of this training session is really measured by how that question is answered—that is, how what has been learned in the session is transferred to the job. Therefore, the training session ends with "experiments in change" . . . activities that the participants can undertake to apply back on the job.

All the essential information you need to conduct this training session follows. Included are an overview of the program and statement of objectives, an outline to view the program at a glance, step-by-step program directions, and general tips for successful facilitation. Prior to conducting the session, you should carefully read through this Leader's Guide and the accompanying Participant's Workbook.

Sixty minutes is a short period of time to conduct effective training. You might wonder how you can do justice to the topic in such a brief period. Our solution is to provide participants with a short article (included in the Participant's Workbook) they can read after the session to provide more detailed information and guidance. Moreover, the inclusion of active training elements can be time-consuming as well. However, if the training elements are well-chosen, a short program can have a substantial impact. Have confidence that our selection of methods will provide maximum impact in a minimum amount of time.

As you prepare yourself to conduct this program, we encourage you to contact us if you have any questions!

Keep 'em active,

Mel Silberman and Freda Hansburg
Active Training
303 Sayre Drive
Princeton, NJ 08540
800–924–8157
mel@activetraining.com
freda@activetraining.com

Visit us on the web at www.activetraining.com

About This Training Program

When people have competing claims, it is very difficult for them to be open to each other's needs and concerns. Often people try to circumvent the discomfort of addressing conflict in an open way, attempting instead to force their solutions on others or avoid the conflict entirely. The underlying tensions are suppressed or ignored, but still simmer below the surface. As a result, resolutions to the conflict are shallow and short-lived. When the next conflict arises, lingering resentments and mistrust may further fuel the flames.

This 60-minute active training program is based on the premise that reaching, or even attempting, a win/win solution requires a willing and active attempt to understand the other person's stated—and unstated—needs. Instead of pushing prematurely for a solution, the most effective approach is to ask good questions aimed at uncovering what is important to the other person so that these issues can become part of the negotiating process.

This design is intended for any participants who experience work-related conflict with virtually anyone, from colleague to customer, from direct report to one's own boss.

Group Size

This program can be conducted with as few as four participants and with as many participants as you like.

Training Objectives

Participants will have the opportunity

- To examine their feelings and current ways of dealing with conflict

- To practice ways to create a climate for win/win resolutions

- To identify opportunities to use conflict-resolution skills within their work context

- To select "experiments in change" at work

Activity	Time	Participant Workbook Page
1. Welcome *A brief review of training objectives*	2 min.	1
2. Word Association 1 *A demonstration that conflict is perceived negatively*	5 min.	2
3. Self-Assessment *An opportunity for participants to assess their approach to conflict*	10 min.	3
4. Comfort with Conflict *An exercise that reveals conflict style*	5 min.	4
5. Four Styles of Conflict *A look at different ways to view conflict*	5 min.	5
6. The Case of the Ugli Oranges *An exercise with a win/win solution*	10 min.	6, 7
7. Getting to Win/Win *A four-step plan*	10 min.	8
8. Experiments in Change *Ways to apply the training*	10 min.	9
9. Word Association 2 *Changing the association*	3 min.	
10. Follow-Up Reading		10 through 16

1. Welcome

(*Time:* 2 minutes; *Materials:* Workbook p. 1)

⟹ Welcome participants and refer them to the objectives of the session on page 1 of their workbooks:

- To examine their feelings and current ways of dealing with conflict

- To practice ways to create a climate for win/win resolutions

- To identify opportunities to use conflict-resolution skills within their work context

- To select "experiments in change" at work

2. Word Association 1

(*Time:* 5 minutes; *Materials:* flip chart or whiteboard, marker, Workbook p. 2)

⟹ Ask participants to complete page 2 in their workbooks. Give them one minute.

⟹ Invite participants to call out some of their associations. Record their words on a flip chart or whiteboard, if available. Stop after ten words.

⟹ Note that most or all the words are negative. (Common negative associations include fighting, battle, unpleasant, nasty, and so forth.)

⟹ Note that we don't have many positive words to describe conflict, yet conflict is natural, normal, and necessary. Point out that as long as there are differences among people, there will be conflicts and competing interests. Yet conflicts can create an opportunity to resolve things that have been brewing under the surface. Conflicts can lead to new ideas and can bring people closer together.

3. Self-Assessment

(*Time:* 10 minutes; *Materials:* Workbook p. 3)

⇒ Invite participants to complete the brief assessment on page 3.

⇒ Pair up participants and ask them to share their ratings with their partners.

⇒ Reconvene the group and request that a few people share which items are a challenge for them. Try to have them identify work-related examples.

4. Comfort with Conflict

(*Time:* 5 minutes; *Materials:* Workbook p. 4)

⇒ Direct participants to workbook page 4, Comfort with Conflict.

⇒ Ask participant to circle the number on the scale for item 1. Poll the group on the ratings selected by participants (for example, *How many of you rated yourself a 4 or 5 on the comfort scale?*)

⇒ Reconvene the pairs from the self-assessment activity and ask them to thumb-wrestle with their partners until one of them wins two out of three rounds (refer to item 2). Then invite them to debrief this short exercise by discussing with each other their responses to the questions on item 3.

⇒ Reconvene the entire group and point out that each of us has habitual ways to deal with conflict . . . that may have been revealed in the manner in which we handled the thumb-wrestling exercise. Some of us like conflict more than others. Some of us are easygoing or cautious or sneaky or downright competitive in conflict situations. However, no one is consistently one style all the time.

5. Four Styles of Conflict

(*Time:* 5 minutes; *Materials:* Workbook p. 5)

⇒ Refer participants to page 5, Four Styles of Conflict, in their workbooks. Ask them to read the descriptions of each style.

⇒ Give some examples of each style to help clarify the differences among them. (You might use political figures, characters on TV programs, and the like as illustrations.)

⇒ Mention that one's conflict style is affected by the context or situation one is in. Ask participants to fill out the bottom section of page 5. Poll the group on their responses. Establish the likelihood that people have different styles in different relationships.

6. The Case of the Ugli Oranges

(*Time:* 10 minutes; *Materials:* Workbook pp. 6 and 7)

⟹ Say: *We are going to do an interesting exercise that will let you put your styles into action.*

⟹ Reconvene the previous pairs.

⟹ Assign one person in each pair the role of Dr. Roland and the other the role of Dr. Jones. Refer "Dr. Roland" to page 6, Role for Dr. Roland, and "Dr. Jones" to page 7, Role for Dr. Jones.

⟹ Say: *I am the owner of 3,000 ugli oranges. After you read about your roles, spend about five minutes meeting with your partner to decide on a course of action. I am strictly interested in making a profit and will sell all the oranges as one lot and only to one of you. Each negotiator can assume that there are no other parties interested in these oranges.*

⟹ Explain: *For the purposes of this exercise, only you and your partner exist. In other words, you are not competing with other pairs who are also assuming the roles of Drs. Roland and Jones.*

⟹ Provide a few minutes for participants to read about their roles. Then begin the exercise and instruct each pair to signal you when they are ready to respond. Stop the exercise after five minutes or when about half the pairs have signaled.

⟹ Invite a pair that has not resolved their differences and ask them to describe the status of the negotiation. Then invite a pair that has achieved a win/win solution to explain their plan.

⟹ Say: *A win/win solution to this conflict was easily obtainable . . . Dr. Roland gets the oranges and takes the rinds and gives the peeled oranges to Dr. Jones, who extracts the juice. As easy as this solution appears, the only way to get there was by putting the parties' real needs on the table. Creating a climate of information sharing is essential to this process. In real life, people remain stuck in a conflict even when there are win/win solutions. Of course, not all conflicts have obvious win/win solutions, but if the parties involved don't communicate with each other, they will never achieve a breakthrough.*

7. Getting to Win/Win

(*Time:* 10 minutes; *Materials:* Workbook p. 8)

⟹ Refer participants to page 8, Getting to Win/Win, in their workbooks.

⟹ Explain that the quotes represent ways you can communicate to someone else that you are willing to work toward an agreement rather than just argue your own position. Invite participants to read page 8.

⇒ Say: *In a typical conflict, each side takes a position, a stand about what they want. For example, one person may want the window in a room to remain open and the other wants the window to be closed. Often, people waste considerable time and effort trying to reconcile positions that are diametrically opposed. In reality, parties in a conflict also hold basic interests, which may be as important or more important to them than the positions they take. For example, the person wanting the window open may be interested in being comfortable while the person wanting the window closed may be interested in securing papers to stay on his or her desk. Interests are our needs, motivations, or reasons for our positions. When we can understand and address the basic needs each side brings to the table, we greatly expand the possibilities for reaching a win/win solution. For example, the person wanting the window open offers a paperweight so that the other person's papers are secured.*

⇒ Pose the following conflict to the group and ask participants how the parties involved might resolve the conflict using the steps on page 8.

Two colleagues have a disagreement about the frequency of meetings. One party believes that meetings should be held on a regular basis. The other party maintains that fixed meetings are unnecessary. The group can discuss most of their business with each other via email and can meet only when it is really required.

⇒ Point out the importance of each party finding out the needs and concerns of the other. Only then would the two colleagues be receptive to brainstorming a creative solution. Give an example: *The agreement could be to lessen the number of fixed meetings because some business can be discussed via email but to maintain a fixed schedule to ensure that face-to-face communication remain an important norm for the group.*

8. Try It: Experiments in Change

(*Time:* 10 minutes; *Materials:* Workbook p. 9)

⇒ Ask participants to look over the choices found on page 9, Experiments in Change, and select at least one they would like to undertake in the next week.

⇒ Invite participants to share their choices with one another.

⇒ Briefly survey the choices made by the entire group.

9. Word Association 2

(*Time:* 3 minutes)

⇒ Remind participants of the negative associations the group made to the word CONFLICT at the beginning of the session.

⇒ Invite participants to think of positive associations ONLY and shout them out when they come to mind. Expect words like opportunity, resolution, meeting needs, brainstorming, and so forth.

⇒ Ask participants whether anyone knows where and how a pearl comes into existence. If not known in the group, explain that sand irritates the inside of an oyster. The oyster, trying to get rid of the irritation, creates a pearl. Point out that, now that they know how to resolve conflict effectively, you hope they can create many "pearls" back on the job.

10. Follow-Up Reading

⇒ Encourage participants to read Resolving Conflict Effectively on pages 10 through 16 outside of the session.

As you conduct this 60-minute training session, bear in mind that active training is especially successful if you do a good job as facilitator. Following are several tips to ensure your success.

Pre-Planning

Your participants will get the most out of this training experience if you follow these general recommendations:

- If possible, have participants do something before they come to the session. For example, provide the article for follow-up reading that accompanies this session to participants for pre-reading instead. Or give participants some questions to think about before the session.

- Customize some of the forms provided for this session so that they reflect as closely as possible the work environment of the participants and the language they would find user-friendly.

- Try to find your own words and illustrate key points with your own examples and personal stories. In addition, alter the sequence of activities when you feel it would be helpful to you in a particular situation. Also, skip details that don't add value for you or the group you are training.

- Encourage participants to identify and discuss their own work situations throughout the session. However, assure them that all conversations are private and confidential.

- Skill practice is a vital part of this program. Role-playing formats are used in the design, such as skits, participant-coached role plays demonstrated by the facilitator, and simultaneous role playing in pairs. Adjust these formats to your needs and the comfort level of your participants.

- As mentioned before, the session ends with "experiments in change" . . . suggested back-on-the-job activities to reinforce your training efforts. Think in advance how you will motivate participants to undertake an experiment in change by offering your availability as a coach or mentor.

Setup

Arrange the physical environment of your 60-minute session to maximize participation and involvement. To accomplish this, use any of the following arrangements:

1. U Shape

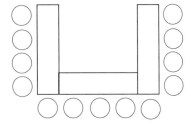

This is an all-purpose setup for up to eighteen participants (three sides of six). (More participants create a setup in which some participants are either too far from you or from each other.) The participants have a reading/writing surface, see you and/or a visual medium easily, and are in face-to-face contact with one another. It's also easy to pair up participants. The arrangement is ideal for distributing handouts quickly to participants since you can enter the U and walk to different points with sets of materials. Be sure there is enough perimeter space in the room so that subgroups of three or more participants can pull back from the tables and face each other.

2. Team Style

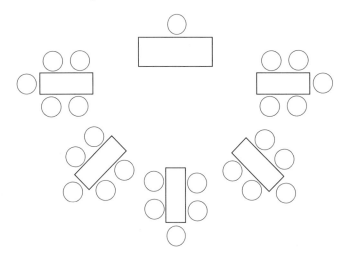

Grouping circular or oblong tables around the classroom enables you to promote team interaction. If you leave the mouth of each table empty, participants can easily see you in the front of the room without having to turn their chairs around. The ideal team table seats six participants. You then can have a subgroup of six, two trios, or three pairs.

3. Conference Table

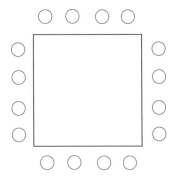

It's best if the table is relatively circular or square. This arrangement minimizes the importance of the leader and maximizes the importance of the group. A rectangular or oval table often creates a sense of formality if you are "at the head of the table," so if you have this type of table, sit in the middle of a wider side. A conference table arrangement works well for pair activity. You need to have perimeter space to create subgroups of three or more.

Facilitating Discussion

Your role during a group discussion is to facilitate the flow of comments from participants. Although it is not necessary to interject after each participant speaks, periodically assisting the group with their contributions can be helpful. Here are some actions to consider:

1. *Paraphrase* what someone has said so that the participant feels understood and the other participants can hear a concise summary of what's been said.

2. *Check your understanding* against the words of a participant or ask a participant to clarify what he or she is saying.

3. *Compliment* an interesting or insightful comment.

4. *Elaborate* on a participant's contribution to the discussion with examples or suggest a new way to view the problem.

5. *Energize* a discussion by quickening the pace, using humor, or, if necessary, prodding the group for more contributions.

6. *Pull together* ideas, showing their relationship to each other.

Facilitating Experiential Activities

When facilitating experiential activities, here are steps to take to be successful:

1. *Explain your objectives.* Participants like to know what is going to happen and why.

2. *Sell the benefits.* Explain why you are doing the activity and share how the activity connects with the other activities before it.

3. *Speak slowly and/or provide visual backup when giving directions.* Make sure the instructions are understandable.

4. *Demonstrate the activity.* If the directions are complicated, let the participants see it in action before they do it.

5. *Divide participants into subgroups before giving further directions.* If you don't, participants may forget the instructions while the groups are being formed.

6. *Inform participants how much time they have.* State the time allotted for the entire activity and then announce periodically how much time remains.

Saving Time

In a 60-minute session, time is at a premium. It's crucial that no time be wasted. Here are things you can do to avoid wasting time:

1. *Start on time.* This act sends a message to latecomers that you're serious. In the event that all of the participants are not yet in the room, begin the class, if you wish, with a discussion or filler activity for which complete attendance is not necessary.

2. *Give clear instructions.* Do not start an activity when participants are confused about what to do. If the directions are complicated, put them in writing.

3. *Prepare visual information ahead of time.* Don't write lecture points on flip charts or the whiteboard while participants watch. Have it prerecorded. Also, decide whether recording participant input is really necessary. If so, don't record the discussion verbatim. Use "headlines" to capture what participants are saying.

4. *Don't let discussions drag on and on.* Express the need to move on, but be sure in later discussion to call on those who didn't have a chance to contribute previously. Or begin a discussion by stating a time limit and suggesting how many contributions time will permit.

5. *Obtain volunteers swiftly.* Don't wait endlessly for them to emerge from the class. You can recruit volunteers before the session begins.

Minimizing Problem Behaviors

Using active training techniques tends to minimize the problems that often plague trainers who rely too heavily on lecture and full group discussion. Nonetheless, difficulties such as monopolizing, distracting, and withdrawing still may occur. Below are interventions you can use:

1. *Signal nonverbally.* Make eye contact with or move closer to participants when they hold private conversations, start to fall asleep, or hide from participation. Press your fingers together (unobtrusively) to signal a wordy participant to finish what he or she is saying. Make a "T" sign (time out) with your fingers to stop unwanted behavior.

2. *Listen actively.* When participants monopolize discussion, go off on a tangent, or argue with you, interject with a summary of their views and then ask others to speak. Or acknowledge the value of their viewpoints and/or invite them to discuss their views with you during a break.

3. *Get your ducks in order.* When the same participants speak up in class while others hold back, pose a question or problem and then ask how many people have a response to it. You should see new hands go up. Call on one of them. The same technique may work when trying to obtain volunteers for role playing.

4. *Invoke participation rules.* From time to time, tell participants that you would like to use rules such as:

   • No laughing during role playing

   • Only participants who have not spoken as yet can participate

   • Build on one another's ideas

   • Speak for yourself, not for others

5. *Use good-natured humor.* One way to deflect difficult behavior is to humor participants. Be careful, however, not to be sarcastic or patronizing. Gently protest the harassment (for example, "Enough, enough for one day!"). Humorously put yourself down instead of the participant (for example, "I guess I'm being stubborn, but. . . .").

6. *Don't take personally the difficulties you encounter.* Remember that many problem behaviors have nothing to do with you. Instead, they are due to personal fears and needs or displaced anger toward someone else. See whether you can pick up cues when this is the case and ask whether participants can put aside the conditions affecting their positive involvement in the training session.

Silberman, M. (2005). *101 ways to make training active (2nd ed.).* San Francisco, CA: Pfeiffer.

Silberman, M. (1998). *Active training (2nd ed.).* San Francisco, CA: Pfeiffer.

Mel Silberman and Freda Hansburg are the authors of *PeopleSmart: Developing Your Interpersonal Intelligence* (Berrett-Koehler, 2000) and *Working PeopleSmart: 6 Strategies for Success* (Berrett-Koehler, 2004). They are also the founders of PeopleSmart Products and Services, an Active Training Company (www.activetraining.com and 800–924–8157).

Mel Silberman is known internationally as a pioneer in the areas of interpersonal skills training, active learning, and team facilitation. As a professor of adult and organizational development at Temple University, he has won two awards for his distinguished teaching. Among his numerous publications are

- *Active Training: A Handbook of Techniques, Designs, Case Examples, and Tips* (Pfeiffer, 1998)

- *The Best of Active Training* (Pfeiffer, 2004)

- *101 Ways to Make Training Active, 2nd ed.* (Pfeiffer, 2005)

- *101 Ways to Make Meetings Active* (Pfeiffer, 1999)

He is also editor of *The ASTD Training and Performance Sourcebook* and *The ASTD Team and Organization Development Sourcebook* (Active Training/ASTD, 2003–2005).

Freda Hansburg is a psychologist in private practice, a training consultant, and an executive coach whose recent clients include BMW of North America, Depository Trust and Clearing Corporation, Merck, and Valero Refining. She has contributed to *The Training and Performance Sourcebook* and made presentations about interpersonal intelligence for ASTD and the OD Network. She is the former director of the Technical Assistance Center, a behavioral health consultation and training program at the University of Medicine and Dentistry of New Jersey.

Pfeiffer Publications Guide

This guide is designed to familiarize you with the various types of Pfeiffer publications. The formats section describes the various types of products that we publish; the methodologies section describes the many different ways that content might be provided within a product. We also provide a list of the topic areas in which we publish.

FORMATS

In addition to its extensive book-publishing program, Pfeiffer offers content in an array of formats, from fieldbooks for the practitioner to complete, ready-to-use training packages that support group learning.

FIELDBOOK Designed to provide information and guidance to practitioners in the midst of action. Most fieldbooks are companions to another, sometimes earlier, work, from which its ideas are derived; the fieldbook makes practical what was theoretical in the original text. Fieldbooks can certainly be read from cover to cover. More likely, though, you'll find yourself bouncing around following a particular theme, or dipping in as the mood, and the situation, dictate.

HANDBOOK A contributed volume of work on a single topic, comprising an eclectic mix of ideas, case studies, and best practices sourced by practitioners and experts in the field.

An editor or team of editors usually is appointed to seek out contributors and to evaluate content for relevance to the topic. Think of a handbook not as a ready-to-eat meal, but as a cookbook of ingredients that enables you to create the most fitting experience for the occasion.

RESOURCE Materials designed to support group learning. They come in many forms: a complete, ready-to-use exercise (such as a game); a comprehensive resource on one topic (such as conflict management) containing a variety of methods and approaches; or a collection of like-minded activities (such as icebreakers) on multiple subjects and situations.

TRAINING PACKAGE An entire, ready-to-use learning program that focuses on a particular topic or skill. All packages comprise a guide for the facilitator/trainer and a workbook for the participants. Some packages are supported with additional media—such as video—or learning aids, instruments, or other devices to help participants understand concepts or practice and develop skills.

- *Facilitator/trainer's guide* Contains an introduction to the program, advice on how to organize and facilitate the learning event, and step-by-step instructor notes. The guide also contains copies of presentation materials—handouts, presentations, and overhead designs, for example—used in the program.

- *Participant's workbook* Contains exercises and reading materials that support the learning goal and serves as a valuable reference and support guide for participants in the weeks and months that follow the learning event. Typically, each participant will require his or her own workbook.

ELECTRONIC CD-ROMs and web-based products transform static Pfeiffer content into dynamic, interactive experiences. Designed to take advantage of the searchability, automation, and ease-of-use that technology provides, our e-products bring convenience and immediate accessibility to your workspace.

METHODOLOGIES

CASE STUDY A presentation, in narrative form, of an actual event that has occurred inside an organization. Case studies are not prescriptive, nor are they used to prove a point; they are designed to develop critical analysis and decision-making skills. A case study has a specific time frame, specifies a sequence of events, is narrative in structure, and contains a plot structure—an issue (what should be/have been done?). Use case studies when the goal is to enable participants to apply previously learned theories to the circumstances in the case, decide what is pertinent, identify the real issues, decide what should have been done, and develop a plan of action.

ENERGIZER A short activity that develops readiness for the next session or learning event. Energizers are most commonly used after a break or lunch to stimulate or refocus the group. Many involve some form of physical activity, so they are a useful way to counter post-lunch lethargy. Other uses include transitioning from one topic to another, where "mental" distancing is important.

EXPERIENTIAL LEARNING ACTIVITY (ELA) A facilitator-led intervention that moves participants through the learning cycle from experience to application (also known as a Structured Experience). ELAs are carefully thought-out designs in which there is a definite learning purpose and intended outcome. Each step—everything that participants do during the activity—facilitates the accomplishment of the stated goal. Each ELA includes complete instructions for facilitating the intervention and a clear statement of goals, suggested group size and timing, materials required, an explanation of the process, and, where appropriate, possible variations to the activity. (For more detail on Experiential Learning Activities, see the Introduction to the *Reference Guide to Handbooks and Annuals*, 1999 edition, Pfeiffer, San Francisco.)

GAME A group activity that has the purpose of fostering team spirit and togetherness in addition to the achievement of a pre-stated goal. Usually contrived—undertaking a desert expedition, for example—this type of learning method offers an engaging means for participants to demonstrate and practice business and interpersonal skills. Games are effective for team building and personal development mainly because the goal is subordinate to the process—the means through which participants reach decisions, collaborate, communicate, and generate trust and understanding. Games often engage teams in "friendly" competition.

ICEBREAKER A (usually) short activity designed to help participants overcome initial anxiety in a training session and/or to acquaint the participants with one another. An icebreaker can be a fun activity or can be tied to specific topics or training goals. While a useful tool in itself, the icebreaker comes into its own in situations where tension or resistance exists within a group.

INSTRUMENT A device used to assess, appraise, evaluate, describe, classify, and summarize various aspects of human behavior. The term used to describe an instrument depends primarily on its format and purpose. These terms include survey, questionnaire, inventory, diagnostic, survey, and poll. Some uses of instruments include providing instrumental feedback to group members, studying here-and-now processes or functioning within a group, manipulating group composition, and evaluating outcomes of training and other interventions.

Instruments are popular in the training and HR field because, in general, more growth can occur if an individual is provided with a method for focusing specifically on his or her own behavior. Instruments also are used to obtain information that will serve as a basis for change and to assist in workforce planning efforts.

Paper-and-pencil tests still dominate the instrument landscape with a typical package comprising a facilitator's guide, which offers advice on administering the instrument and interpreting the collected data, and an initial set of instruments. Additional instruments are available separately. Pfeiffer, though, is investing heavily in e-instruments. Electronic instrumentation provides effortless distribution and, for larger groups particularly, offers advantages over paper-and-pencil tests in the time it takes to analyze data and provide feedback.

LECTURETTE A short talk that provides an explanation of a principle, model, or process that is pertinent to the participants' current learning needs. A lecturette is intended to establish a common language bond between the trainer and the participants by providing a mutual frame of reference. Use a lecturette as an introduction to a group activity or event, as an interjection during an event, or as a handout.

MODEL A graphic depiction of a system or process and the relationship among its elements. Models provide a frame of reference and something more tangible, and more easily remembered, than a verbal explanation. They also give participants something to "go on," enabling them to track their own progress as they experience the dynamics, processes, and relationships being depicted in the model.

ROLE PLAY A technique in which people assume a role in a situation/scenario: a customer service rep in an angry-customer exchange, for example. The way in which the role is approached is then discussed and feedback is offered. The role play is often repeated using a different approach and/or incorporating changes made based on feedback received. In other words, role playing is a spontaneous interaction involving realistic behavior under artificial (and safe) conditions.

SIMULATION A methodology for understanding the interrelationships among components of a system or process. Simulations differ from games in that they test or use a model that depicts or mirrors some aspect of reality in form, if not necessarily in content. Learning occurs by studying the effects of change on one or more factors of the model. Simulations are commonly used to test hypotheses about what happens in a system—often referred to as "what if?" analysis—or to examine best-case/worst-case scenarios.

THEORY A presentation of an idea from a conjectural perspective. Theories are useful because they encourage us to examine behavior and phenomena through a different lens.

TOPICS

The twin goals of providing effective and practical solutions for workforce training and organization development and meeting the educational needs of training and human resource professionals shape Pfeiffer's publishing program. Core topics include the following:

Leadership & Management

Communication & Presentation

Coaching & Mentoring

Training & Development

e-Learning

Teams & Collaboration

OD & Strategic Planning

Human Resources

Consulting

What will you find on pfeiffer.com?

- The best in workplace performance solutions for training and HR professionals

- Downloadable training tools, exercises, and content

- Web-exclusive offers

- Training tips, articles, and news

- Seamless on-line ordering

- Author guidelines, information on becoming a Pfeiffer Affiliate, and much more

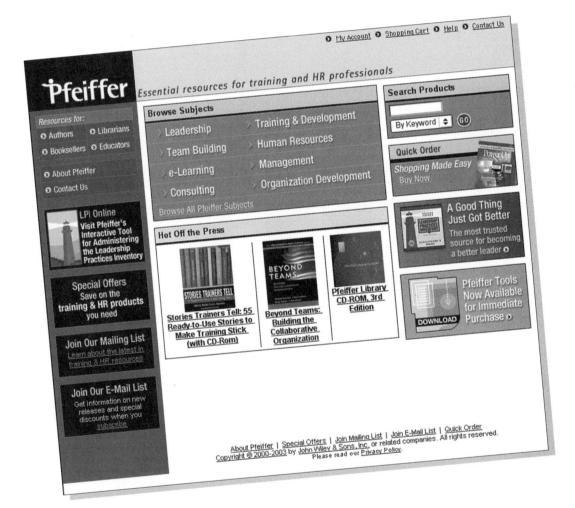

Discover more at www.pfeiffer.com

Customer Care

Have a question, comment, or suggestion? Contact us! We value your feedback and we want to hear from you.

For questions about this or other Pfeiffer products, you may contact us by:

E-mail: **customer@wiley.com**

Mail: **Customer Care Wiley/Pfeiffer**
         10475 Crosspoint Blvd.
         Indianapolis, IN 46256

Phone: **(US) 800-274-4434** (Outside the US: 317-572-3985)

Fax: **(US) 800-569-0443** (Outside the US: 317-572-4002)

To order additional copies of this title or to browse other Pfeiffer products, visit us online at **www.pfeiffer.com**.

For **Technical Support** questions call **(800) 274-4434.**

For authors guidelines, log on to www.pfeiffer.com and click on "Resources for Authors."

If you are . . .

A **college bookstore, a professor, an instructor, or work in higher education** and you'd like to place an order or request an exam copy, please contact jbreview@wiley.com.

A **general retail bookseller** and you'd like to establish an account or speak to a local sales representative, contact Melissa Grecco at 201-748-6267 or mgrecco@wiley.com.

An **exclusively on-line bookseller**, contact Amy Blanchard at 530-756-9456 or ablanchard @wiley.com or Jennifer Johnson at 206-568-3883 or jjohnson@wiley.com, both of our Online Sales department.

A **librarian or library representative**, contact John Chambers in our Library Sales department at 201-748-6291 or jchamber@wiley.com.

A **reseller, training company/consultant, or corporate trainer**, contact Charles Regan in our Special Sales department at 201-748-6553 or cregan@wiley.com.

A **specialty retail distributor** (includes specialty gift stores, museum shops, and corporate bulk sales), contact Kim Hendrickson in our Special Sales department at 201-748-6037 or khendric@wiley.com.

Purchasing for the **Federal government**, contact Ron Cunningham in our Special Sales department at 317-572-3053 or rcunning@wiley.com.

Purchasing for a **State or Local government**, contact Charles Regan in our Special Sales department at 201-748-6553 or cregan@wiley.com.

TRAINING SOLUTIONS
are just a lunch hour away!

Mel Silberman is synonymous with Active Training. Thousands upon thousands of trainers look to him for sage advice on teaching adults the way they learn best—by doing.

Now you can have the most effective, to-the-point, immediate training solutions for some of the most common training topics, all based on the successful Active Training method: proven to enhance learning and retention. The 60-Minute Active Training Series is ideal for experienced practitioners as well as team leaders and the occasional trainer—anyone who needs to provide on-the-job group training or lunch and learn sessions.

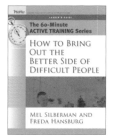

Leader's Guide
ISBN 0-7879-7354-8

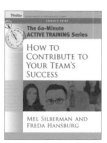

Leader's Guide
ISBN 0-7879-7353-X

Leader's Guide
ISBN 0-7879-7350-5

Leader's Guide
ISBN 0-7879-7351-3

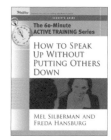

Leader's Guide
ISBN 0-7879-7355-6

Each title in The 60-Minute Active Training Series has a Leader's Guide and Participant's Workbook. There are no other materials to buy. With The 60-Minute Active Training Series, solutions to your training problems are just a lunch-hour away!

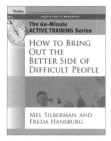

Participant's Workbook
ISBN 0-7879-7358-0

Participant's Workbook
ISBN 0-7879-7357-2

Participant's Workbook
ISBN 0-7879-7352-1

Participant's Workbook
ISBN 0-7879-7356-4

Participant's Workbook
ISBN 0-7879-7359-9

**To order these, or any Pfeiffer title, visit www.pfeiffer.com
or call toll-free 800-245-6217**

The 60-Minute ACTIVE TRAINING Series
HOW TO RESOLVE CONFLICT EFFECTIVELY
LEADER'S GUIDE

Too often, in situations of conflict, people seek victory rather than agreement. Resolving conflict successfully means taking a different approach where both parties benefit—creating a win-win situation. *How to Resolve Conflict Effectively, Leader's Guide* from the popular *60-Minute Active Training Series* offers facilitators a ready-made, effective one-hour program that teaches participants the skills they need to successfully resolve conflict and create win-win situations. Specifically, participants will learn how to

- **Get tension right out on the table**
- **Figure out what's bothering the other person**
- **Communicate the real, underlying concerns**

The 60-Minute Active Training Series offers targeted learning solutions designed around the Active Training method pioneered by Mel Silberman. Each title in the series focuses on a core interpersonal or team-related skill and can be facilitated in the workplace, or as part of a formal training program.

Active Training is one of the most significant learning methods to emerge in the last thirty years. The effectiveness of the method is due in large part to the connections made between learning and participant's own, personal experience. It's an approach that enhances learning transfer by motivating participants to immediately apply what they learn back in the workplace.

THE AUTHORS

MEL SILBERMAN is president of Active Training in Princeton, New Jersey, a consulting firm that provides courses on active training techniques, interpersonal intelligence, and team facilitation. He is the author or coauthor of the best-selling books, *Active Training*, *101 Ways to Make Training Active*, and *PeopleSmart*.

FREDA HANSBURG is vice president of Active Training and coauthor of *PeopleSmart*.

"In less time than it takes to go out to lunch, participants gain valuable knowledge, master practical techniques, and acquire skills immediately applicable to personal or professional situations. Practical, participative, producing results—what more could any trainer or performance-improvement technologist want?"
—Elaine Biech, author, *Training for Dummies*

COLLECT ALL THE BOOKS IN *The 60-Minute Active Training Series* **FOR YOUR PROFESSIONAL LIBRARY**

How to Bring Out the Better Side of Difficult People, Leader's Guide and *Participant's Workbook*
How to Encourage Constructive Feedback from Others, Leader's Guide and *Participant's Workbook*
How to Contribute to Your Team's Success, Leader's Guide and *Participant's Workbook*
How to Speak Up Without Putting Others Down, Leader's Guide and *Participant's Workbook*

TRAINING AND HUMAN RESOURCE DEVELOPMENT

Discover more at
www.pfeiffer.com

Pfeiffer®
An Imprint of
WILEY

ISBN 0-7879-7351-3

90000

9 780787 973513

Pfeiffer *Essential resources for training and HR professionals*

The 60-Minute ACTIVE TRAINING Series

How to Encourage Constructive Feedback from Others

Mel Silberman and Freda Hansburg

About This Resource

Why is this topic important?

In many organizations, feedback is often withheld because a person is not sure the potential receiver wants or would appreciate the feedback. In addition, a person may feel that he or she is overstepping the bounds, especially if the receiver is a colleague or boss. Or maybe the receiver would become angry, or even seek reprisal. Finally, the person may just not want the hassle. Because feedback on the job can be a scarce commodity, it is important for people to understand that waiting for feedback from others isn't enough. Instead, they need to encourage feedback from a wide circle of people.

What can you achieve with this resource?

This is a guide for the person who wishes to facilitate a training program that motivates individuals at any level within the organization to seek feedback from others. It is ideal for participants who want to take responsibility for their own growth and development . . . regardless of their job or role.

Although brief, the program is not a leader-centered presentation or merely an hour of group discussion. Instead, participants are engaged in short activities that heighten their awareness of their current attitudes and behaviors, inspire them to adopt new ones, and provide them with concrete suggestions that can be used immediately back on the job.

How is this resource organized?

The training program can be conducted in one hour (the length can be extended with a more leisurely pace) without making concessions to the extra time that participatory training sessions usually require. It features "active training" techniques in which lecturing is minimized and learning activity is maximized. The 60-minute format allows the facilitator to provide effective training in a brief time period. As a result, busy employees can attend a training session without disrupting their work day. The active training techniques used in this program are designed to increase participation, enliven learning, deepen retention, and encourage application.

The program can be conducted with as few as four participants and yet also functions well for a larger group. Participants can be drawn from different parts of an organization or be members of an intact unit or team.